LIMA IS LOOKING FOR A FRIEND

NANETTE CALDWELL

Copyright © 2020 by Nanette Caldwell.

ISBN-978-1-6485-8217-2

All rights reserved. No part of this book may be reproduced or transmitted in any form or by any means, electronic or mechanical, including photocopying, recording, or by any information storage and retrieval system, without permission in writing from the copyright owner.

The views expressed in this work are solely those of the author and do not necessarily reflect the views of the publisher, and the publisher hereby disclaims any responsibility for them.

Matchstick Literary
1-888-306-8885
orders@matchliterary.com

Once, there was a cute little male dog.

We got him in our home when he was only about 8 weeks old.

He was the joy of our family!

Every day, when he woke up, he wanted to play.

He became the center of our attention because we did not have a baby in our home.

As he grew day by day, we had to train him to live in our house.

To begin with, we potty trained him!

We also set a time for him to eat and play.

As time went by, he got into a habit of chewing on our furniture.

It was terrible!

All our family members had a responsibility towards Lima.

In the morning, mother would take him to the bathroom.

Then she would feed him breakfast.

After breakfast Lima would go back to his cage in the bedroom.

He would then take his nap.

As soon as he woke up,

Lima slept in the bedroom in the cage at night.

When Lima was six months old, he became very lonely.

He was the only dog in the house!

Dad would take him out to the porch and he would look out for someone walking a dog.

After watching for some time, he would get disappointed again.

One summer day, a 15 year old boy walking with his pet, got Lima excited.

He thought it was a dog but it turned out to be a Persian cat!

Then he went back to his cage and stayed there.

Dad felt sorry for Lima.

www.ingramcontent.com/pod-product-compliance
Lightning Source LLC
Chambersburg PA
CBHW042252100526
44587CB00002B/110